AF602018

Giulio R. M. Maffii

COPIA

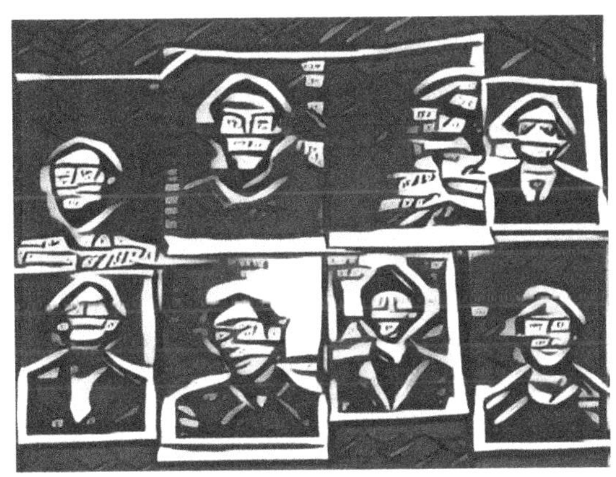

Wet Cement Press

ISBN 979-8-9918692-9-4

English version and cover image by Giulio R. M. Maffii

Wet Cement Press
450 N. Canton Rd.
Canton, NC 28716
Berkeley, CA 94707

www.wetcementpress.com

For my children,
my only copies that turned out better than the original

I
(one)

Le nombre est dans l'individu
—C. Baudelaire

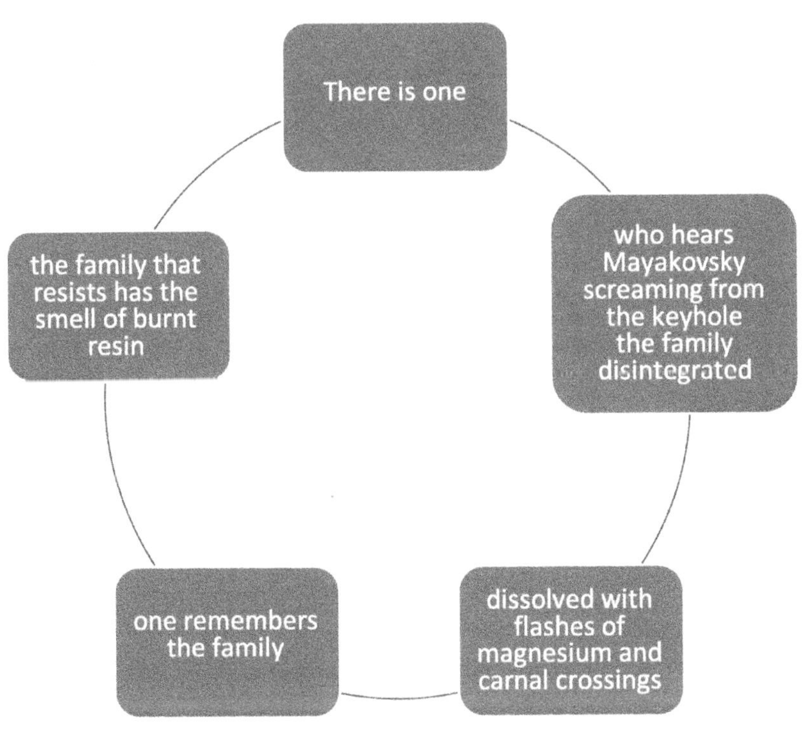
There is one
who hears Mayakovsky screaming from the keyhole the family disintegrated
dissolved with flashes of magnesium and carnal crossings
one remembers the family
the family that resists has the smell of burnt resin

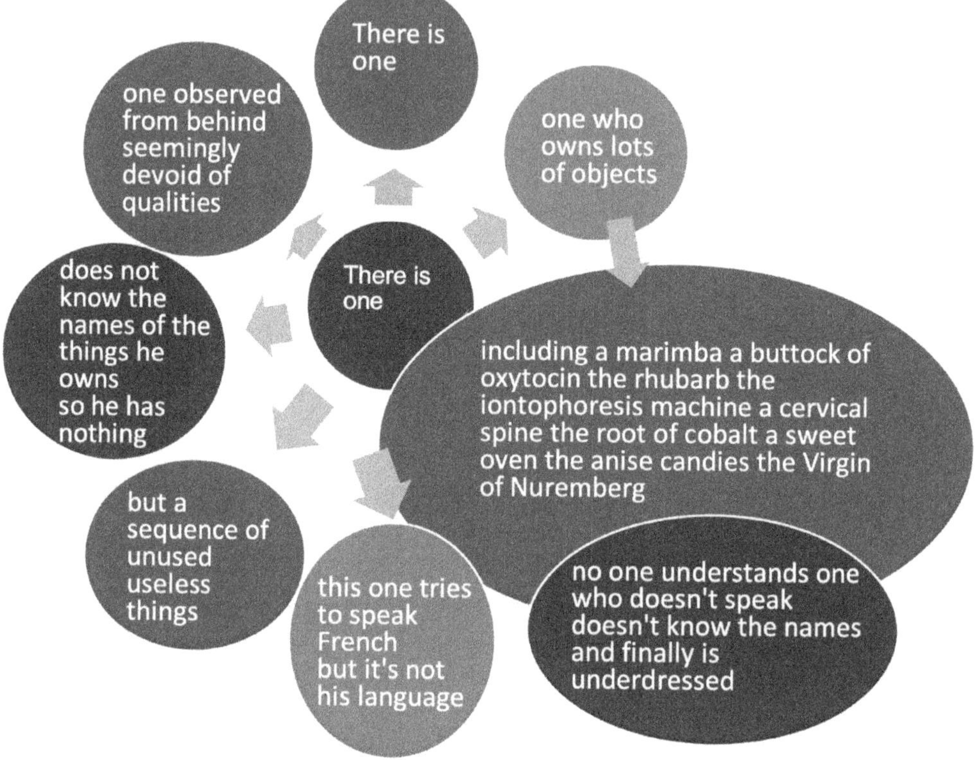

There is one

There is one

one who owns lots of objects

including a marimba a buttock of oxytocin the rhubarb the iontophoresis machine a cervical spine the root of cobalt a sweet oven the anise candies the Virgin of Nuremberg

no one understands one who doesn't speak doesn't know the names and finally is underdressed

this one tries to speak French
but it's not his language

but a sequence of unused useless things

does not know the names of the things he owns
so he has nothing

one observed from behind seemingly devoid of qualities

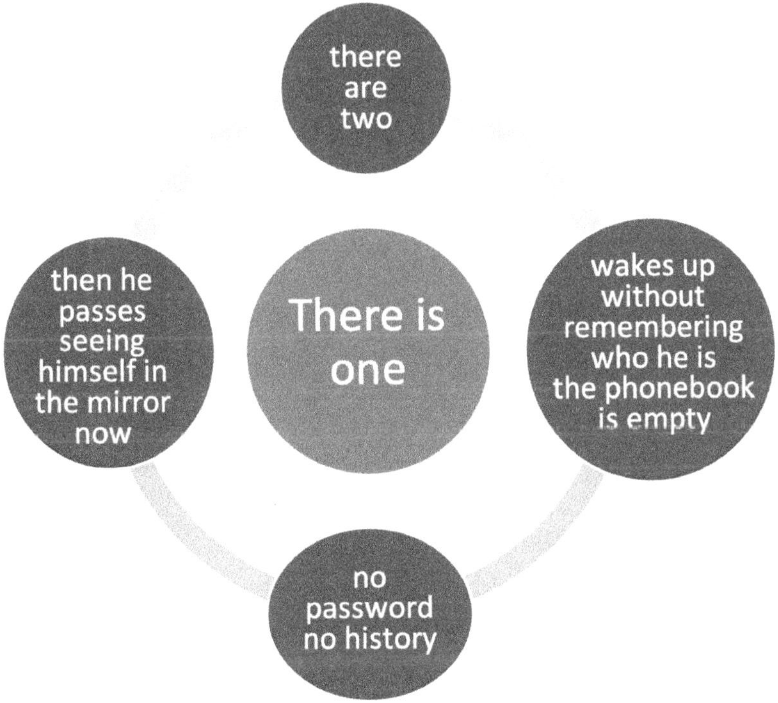

There is one

there are two

wakes up without remembering who he is the phonebook is empty

no password no history

then he passes seeing himself in the mirror now

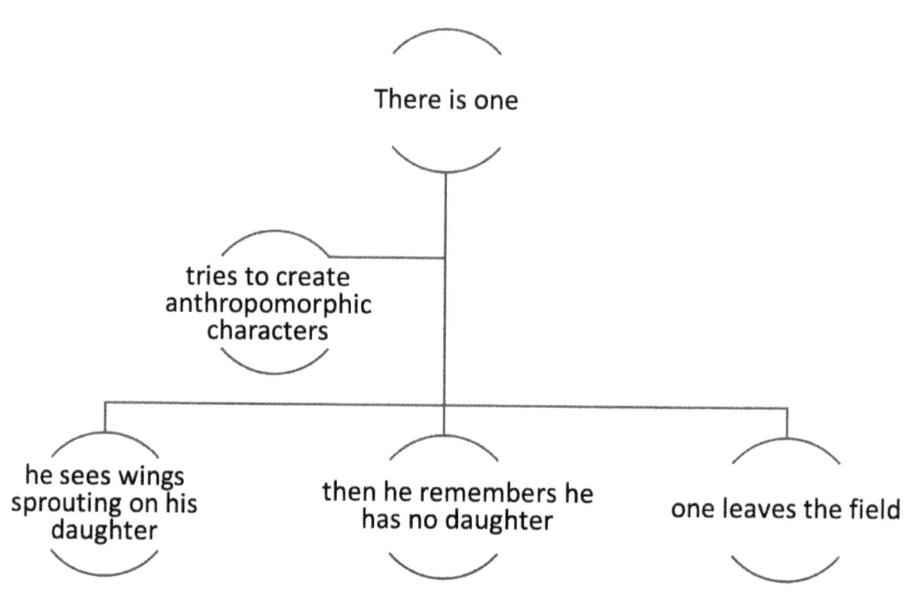
There is one
tries to create anthropomorphic characters
he sees wings sprouting on his daughter
then he remembers he has no daughter
one leaves the field

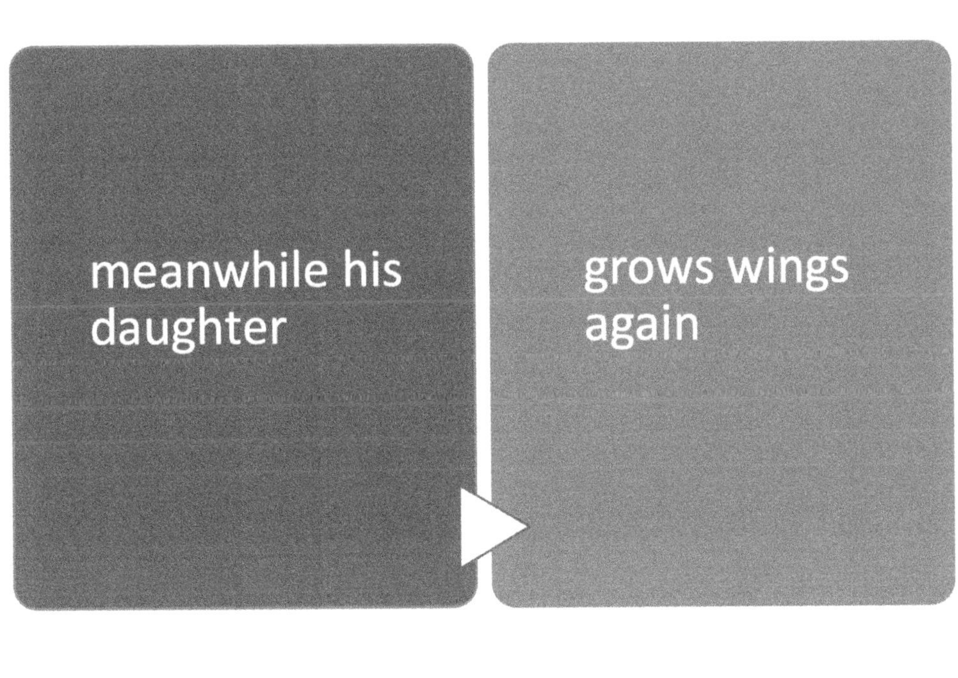
meanwhile his daughter
grows wings again

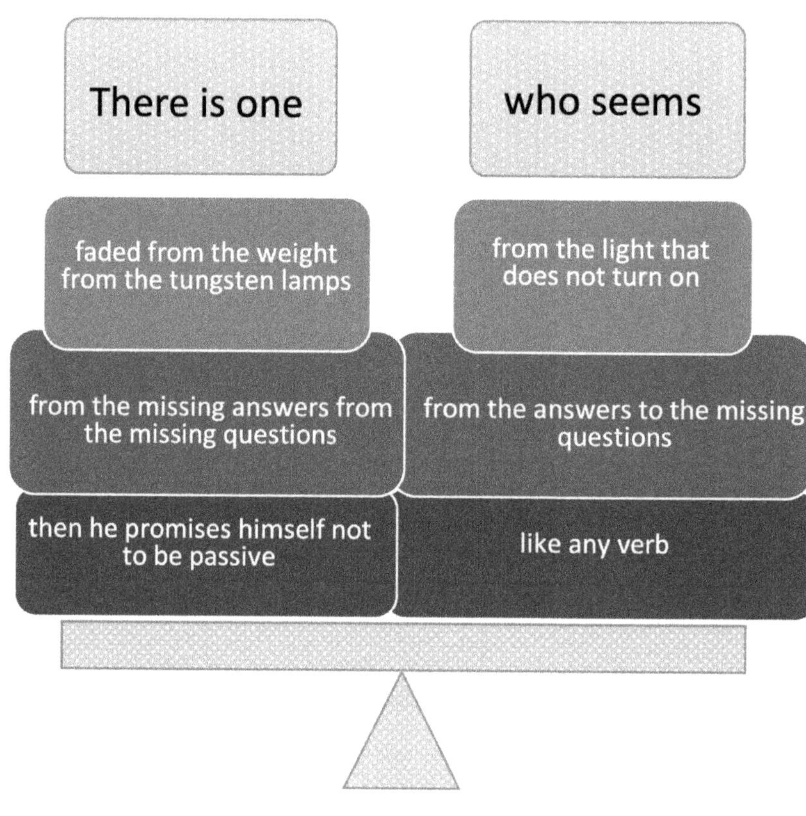
There is one
who seems
faded from the weight from the tungsten lamps
from the light that does not turn on
from the missing answers from the missing questions
from the answers to the missing questions
then he promises himself not to be passive
like any verb

a neutral declension an invisible neutrino
then he tells himself that next time

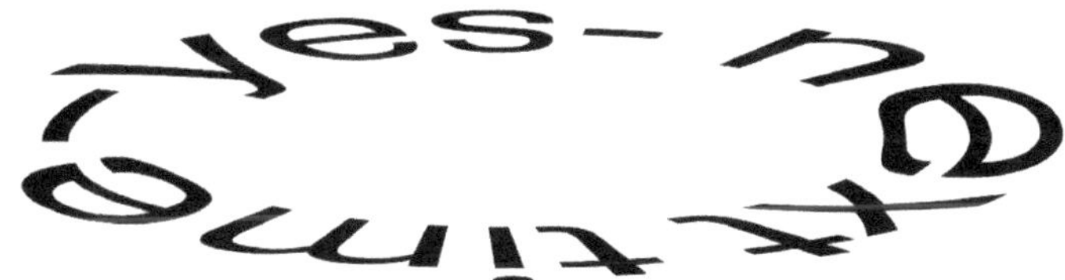

-yes- next time

There is one
wondering what he will do
he asks himself after passing a sliding door
the bus stop in the rush hour
in front of the perspective line of a suburban avenue
he asks himself in front of an apple
of a dying father at the cut inflicted by a mad god
from a mad person from an idling engine
One wonders what to do
then takes a few pills
even pills do something
plans a trip
buys new glasses
sees people in line
he will go through life waiting for hols

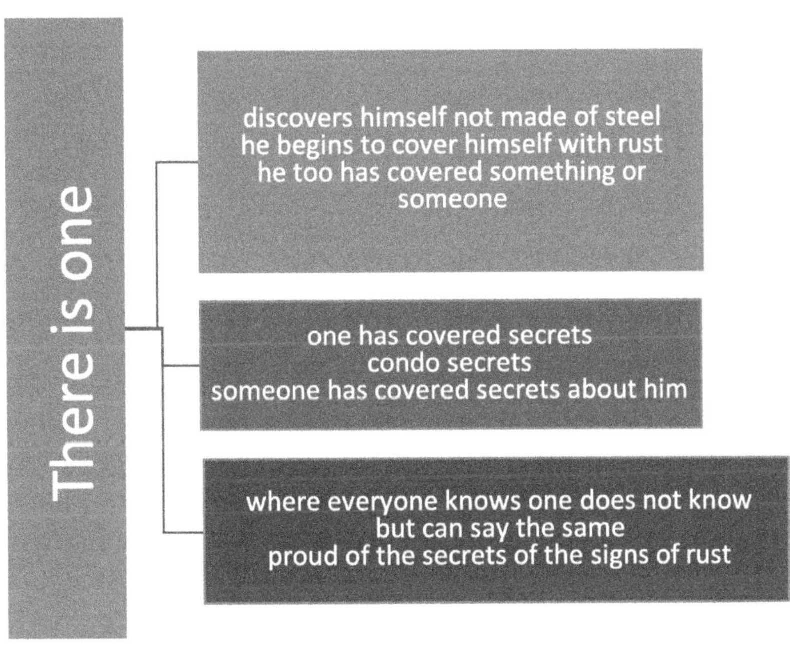

proud of time necessary to go upstairs in the condo

There is one
remembers when
thirty years ago
he was twenty
remembers some
people he has known
whom he hasn't seen
for thirty years

He thinks he will no longer
be able to see them
that some are dead
that others would not
recognize him
that he would not
recognize them

He thinks that knowing each
other is not enough
to recognize each other
or not to die

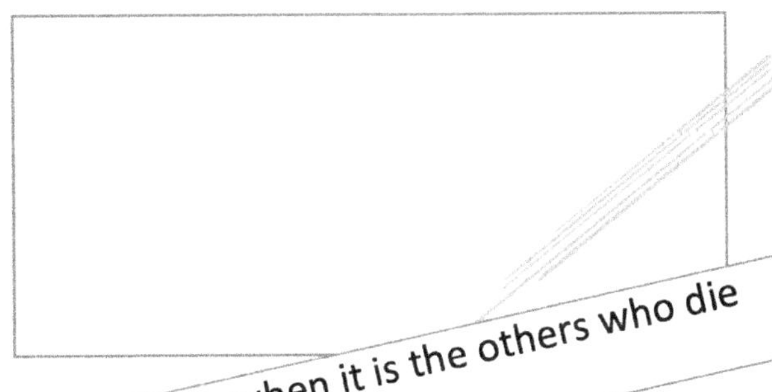

One is happy when it is the others who die

There is one

who always plays Scrabble
he can't write his name

the letters are never enough
he also suffers from hyperlexia

like many readers

he has no name but likes

to play Scrabble

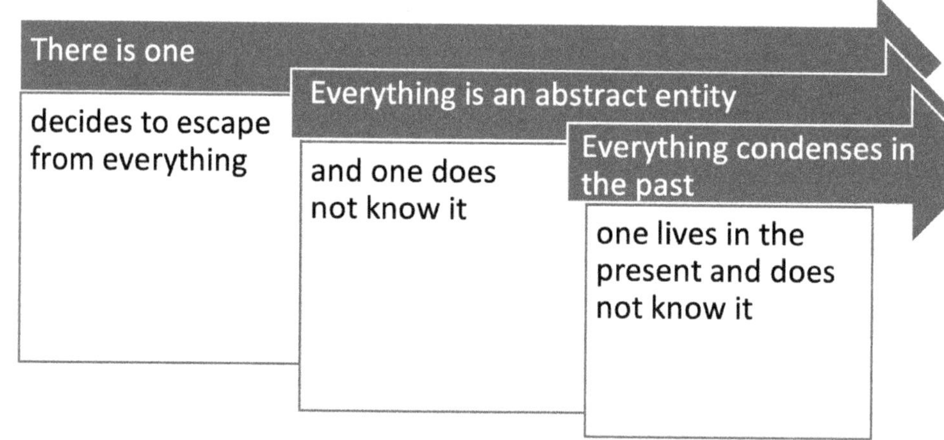
There is one
decides to escape from everything
Everything is an abstract entity
and one does not know it
Everything condenses in the past
one lives in the present and does not know it

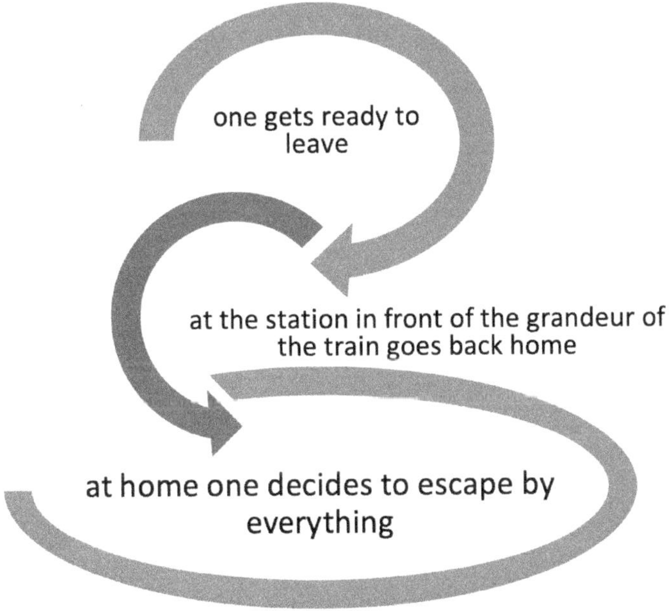

one gets ready to leave

at the station in front of the grandeur of the train goes back home

at home one decides to escape by everything

a draft from the window
blows in all the rooms
residues mixed with fine dust

spreading painful speeches
delays betrayals Christmas
parties a stain on the pillow
the clogged shower

There is one

a video of a few years ago
the cold colder than an office
and marble and
mass-produced furniture

two sleepy tiger mosquitoes
the last one salary
hardcore hot spot Jesus
of Nazareth

II

(unknows)

i passanti, scuri e bassi, pesanti: avvolti nel fazzoletto sopra la faccia
—A. Spatola

There is one
vomits something from the mouth
vomits the rib cage
in few words vomits
his own ribs he was born from

according to a mistakenly Western tradition
There are many passers-by in the rush hour
they tilt and do not stop to look at
one who throws up pieces of arteries on the street
and pieces of road from the arteries

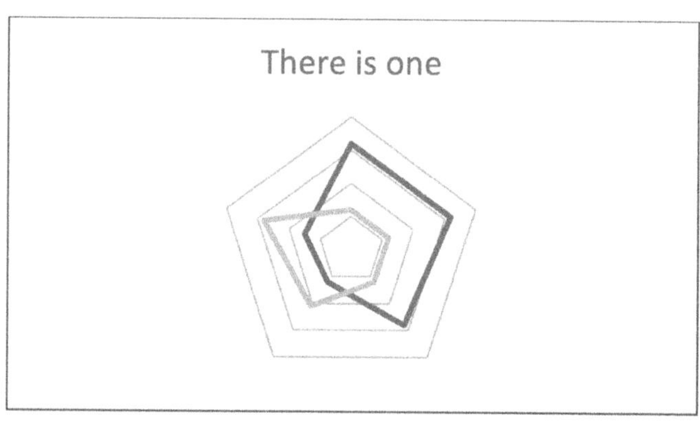

is a besieged
Infinite letters pass from a point
any point
stop and comma fixed in his pride
the iconoclastic siege is ∞
one is not prepared to resist
even the siege shows cracks

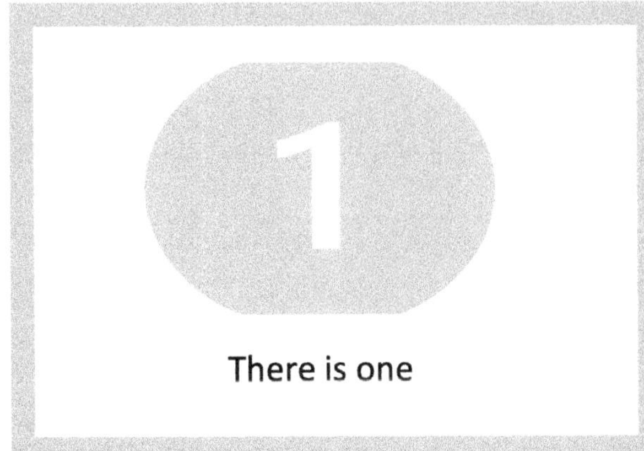

There is one

Reads in the dreams of
those sleeping next to
him perhaps it is not
correct to say “he
reads” he sees them
He sees many things
some escape him
there are many things
that escape not only
people or kings
He sees someone
making love in a dream
with the person who
sleeps next to him
There are so many
things that escape

There is one

Writes the sentences heard on the street
people's literary bulimia
he writes on the buses of the unknowns
in the center in the suburbs he writes

There will be another time
Do you want my seat?
Here once there were
Do you know the story of?

Prepare in time for the stop
the paper will run out and
the ink too
the environmentalists want
to beat up Gutenberg

No one will be able to
do the Rorschach
let alone who writes
the sentences
heard on the street or
by others

The devil
take the
hindmost

The devil
take

Let’s hope for the best
Let’s hope

Let’s hope for the best
Let’s hope

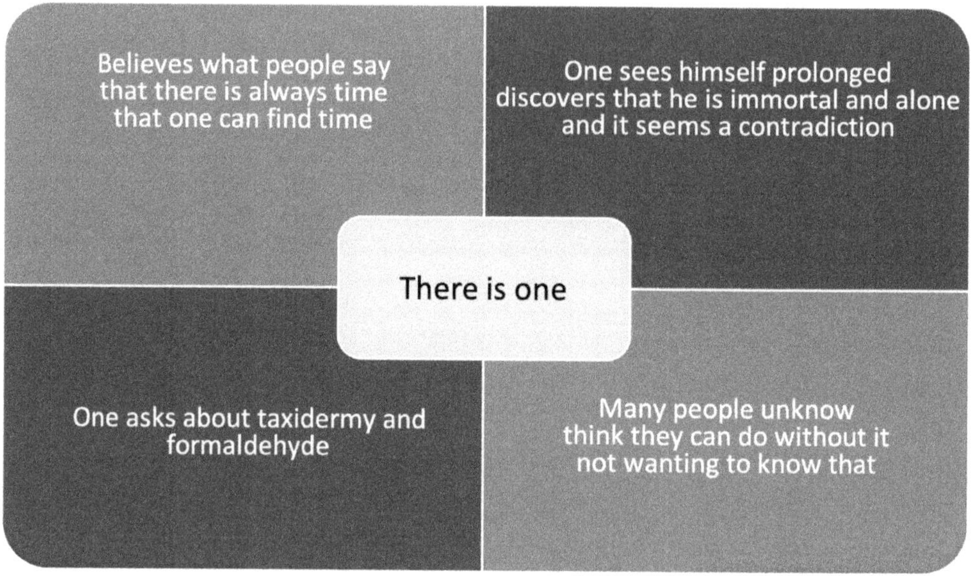

Believes what people say
that there is always time
that one can find time

One sees himself prolonged
discovers that he is immortal and alone
and it seems a contradiction

There is one

One asks about taxidermy and
formaldehyde

Many people unknow
think they can do without it
not wanting to know that

(That one can find his time)

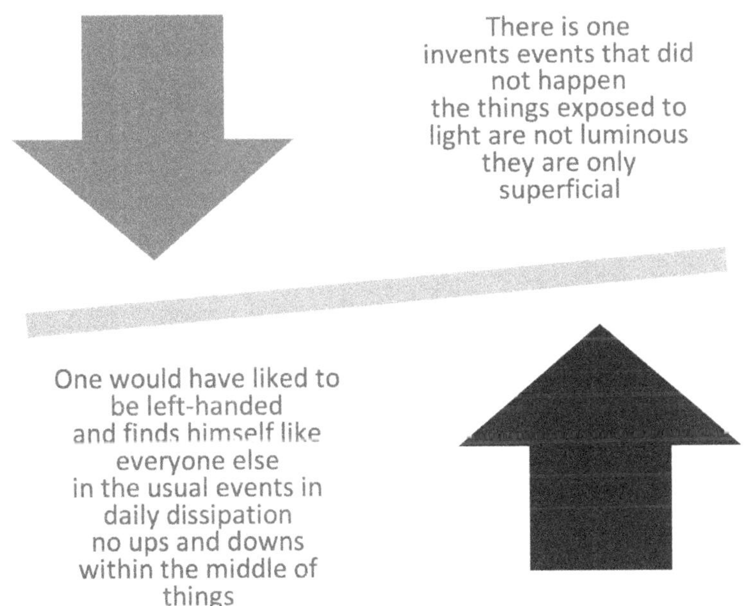

4 zones are defined technically called bands of frequency in the audio

There is one

- the things the events disperse him
  the things the events the beams disperse themselves
- the rooms the objects the joints on the floor
  in the end they're indifferent

The step towards the kitchen is indifferent to the floor

- what resounds behind is indifference
  to any of which one shows ass
  one saves Christmas lights
- the crumpled cup
  the similarities in the leaden mirror

One reminds the beautiful part of childhood
the first lips in a gym locker room

- winter almost never lies
  and sends us postcards from hibernation
- one thinks that bodies are goods
  the bodies do consume in the undifferentiated waste

There is one
often wonders what
they do in the offices
what paperwork is

how they can let time
pass between neon light
and people
people are nothing but
the unknowns

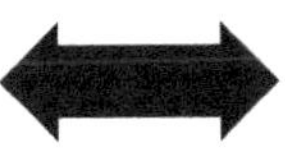

the unknowns fill Google
photos maps with their faces
always hidden

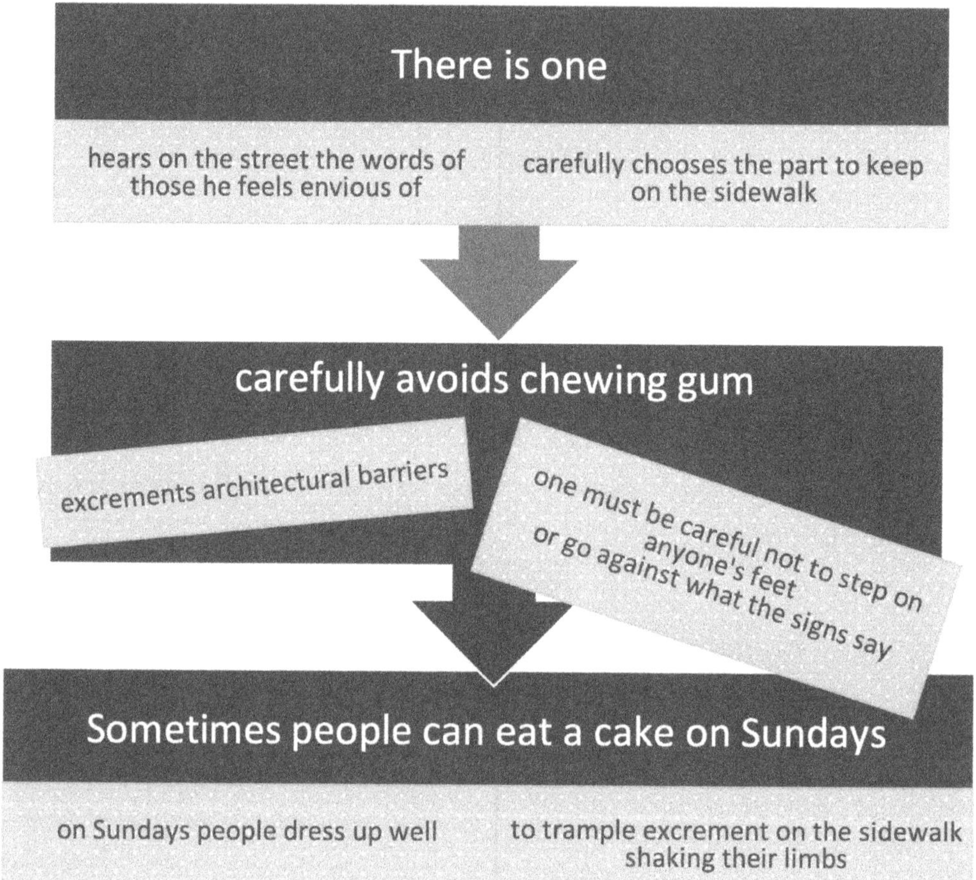

There is one

hears on the street the words of those he feels envious of

carefully chooses the part to keep on the sidewalk

carefully avoids chewing gum

excrements architectural barriers

one must be careful not to step on anyone's feet
or go against what the signs say

Sometimes people can eat a cake on Sundays

on Sundays people dress up well

to trample excrement on the sidewalk shaking their limbs

There is one
wonders what he did wrong
the same question echoes

in the condominium stairs
in the residences in the historic center
in the isolated country villas

even in the chalets with snow around
and the blessed faces of Christmas of goods and banks
the same question echoes

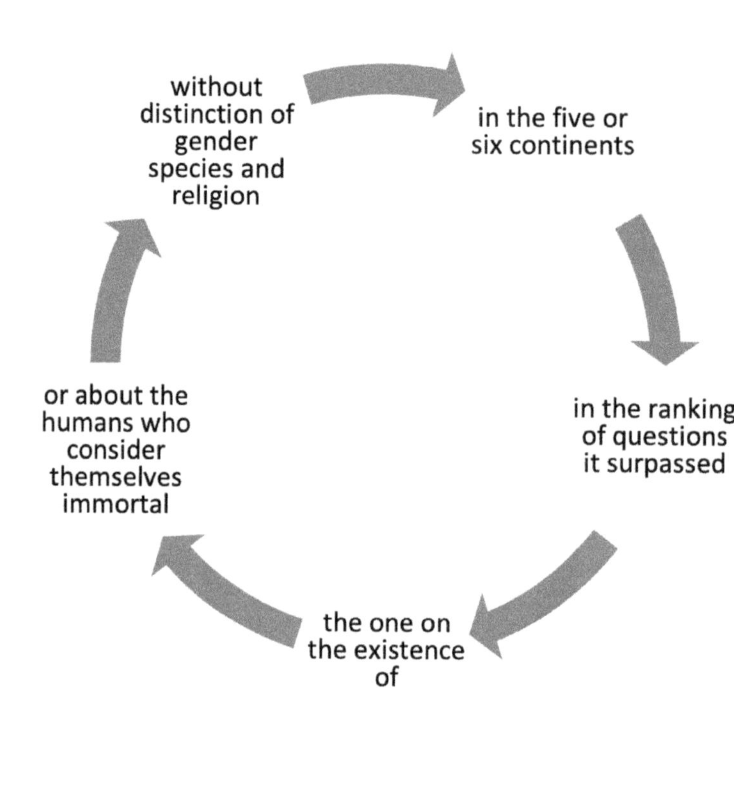
without distinction of gender species and religion
in the five or six continents
in the ranking of questions it surpassed
the one on the existence of
or about the humans who consider themselves immortal

There is one
who has spent a long time
looking for that thing they call by a
name
it was and/or other

and also an ellipsis
and also
Then one day he realizes that
he reciprocates with passion and
moustache and he bumps his hard belly

against a hard belly
that is nothing other than
or one with Playboy

- the beautiful mags of
once upon a time -
or something else
altogether

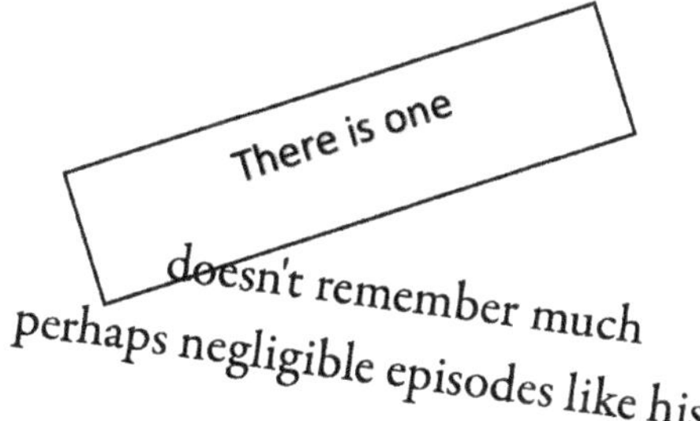

doesn't remember much
perhaps negligible episodes like his life

the involuntary dramaturgy
the 21,600 breaths a day
multiplied by (?)

Perhaps he remembers something about music
but not even much

he is an unknown person
a sin cara
one lost among the unknowns
just like so many like all of us as you want

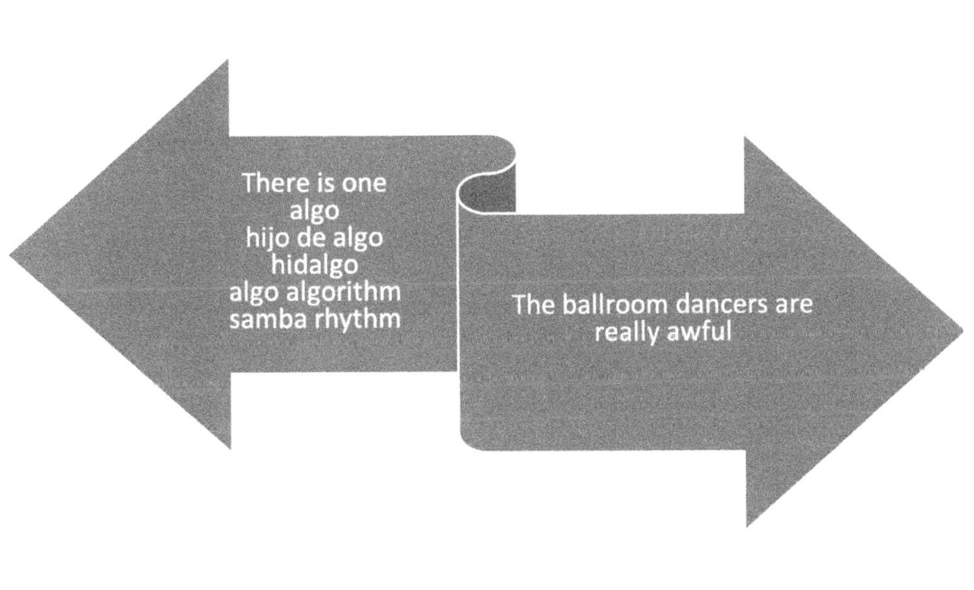
There is one
algo
hijo de algo
hidalgo
algo algorithm
samba rhythm
The ballroom dancers are
really awful

is still motionless
observing
the unknowns going
up and down the
stairs in
thunderstorms
in the umpteenth
shopping center
where the nameless
take refuge
identified by c 14
by a metal timepiece

There
is one

next to the chessboard
they go up and down
someone remains inclined
to the sides one doesn’t
know if those who go up
are more than the ones
who go down and leans
over to find out then
remembers he can't count

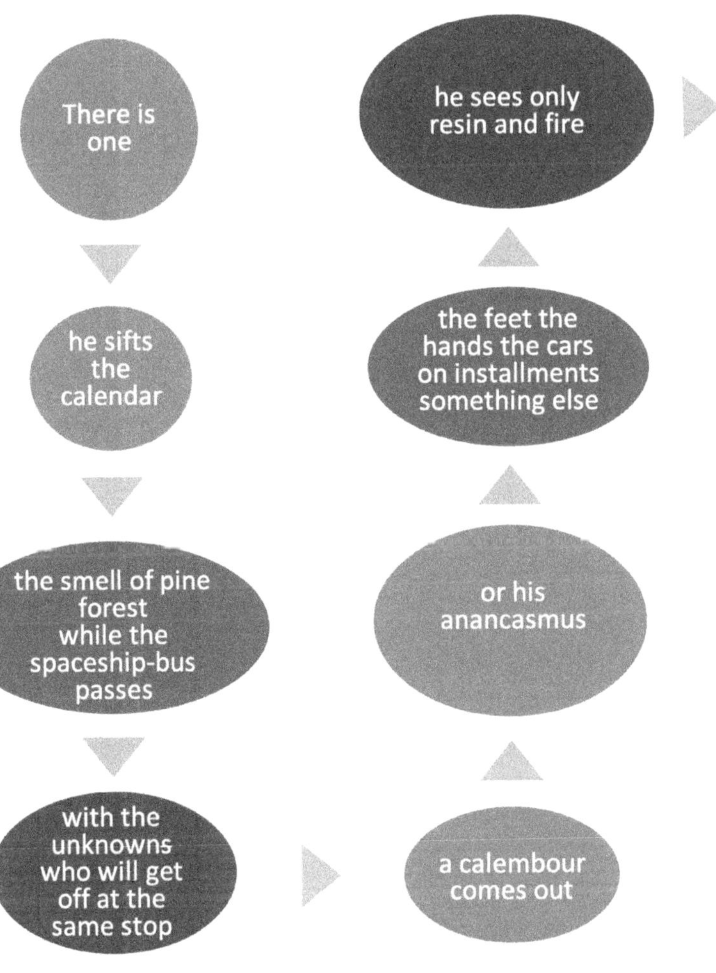

There is one
he sifts the calendar
the smell of pine forest
while the spaceship-bus passes
with the unknowns who will get off at the same stop
a calembour comes out
or his anancasmus
the feet the hands the cars on installments something else
he sees only resin and fire
In case of -breaking the winner-

III

(bourgeois)

Ma se cambia la stagione che ne farò del lavoro?
Delle nove ore di terra cotta dipinte nei luoghi deputati:
scale ascensori salotti d'attesa e soprattutto
finestre chiuse contro vento?
—L. Ballerini

There is one
when he dreams he always dreams

one discovers that literature is the scam of X-ray glasses

than one of the infinite worlds of the infinite ways of the infinite seas

then in a dream Borges appears to one
who looks into the distance
and wears contact lenses

and discovers it in a dream that it is nothing else

of the average infinites
of the infinite evil
and so on until the end
of the driveway

surrounded by sheet metal barriers

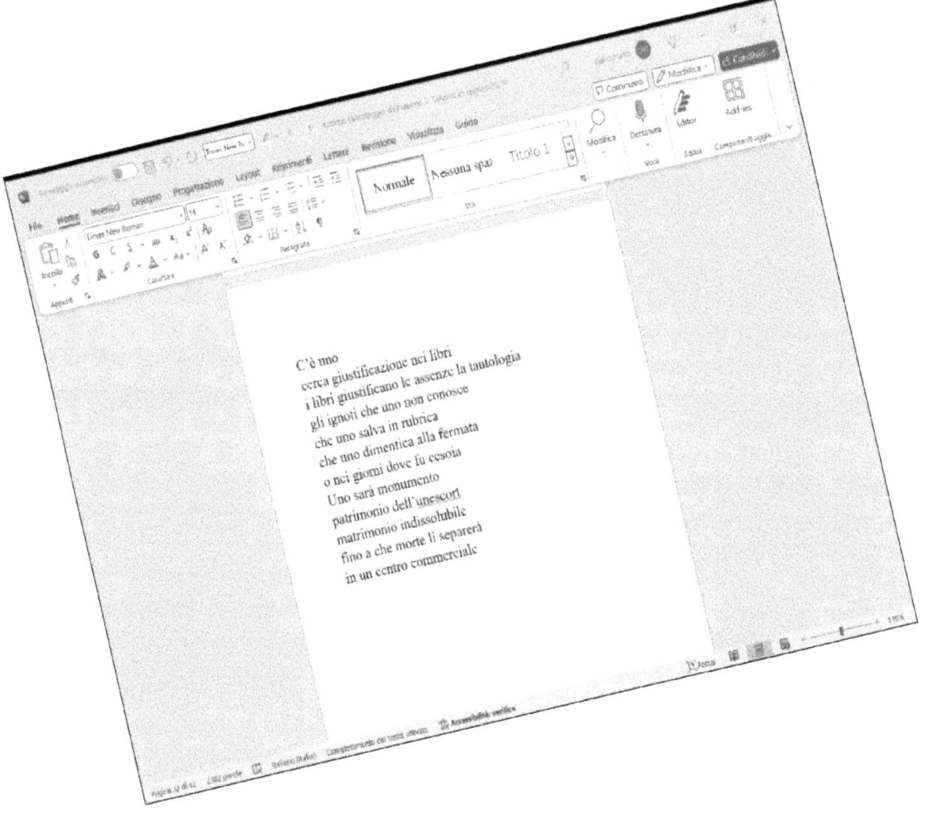
C'è uno
cerca giustificazione nei libri
i libri giustificano le assenze la tautologia
gli ignoti che uno non conosce
che uno salva in rubrica
che uno dimentica alla fermata
o nei giorni dove fu cesoia
Uno sarà monumento
patrimonio dell'unescort
matrimonio indissolubile
fino a che morte li separerà
in un centro commerciale

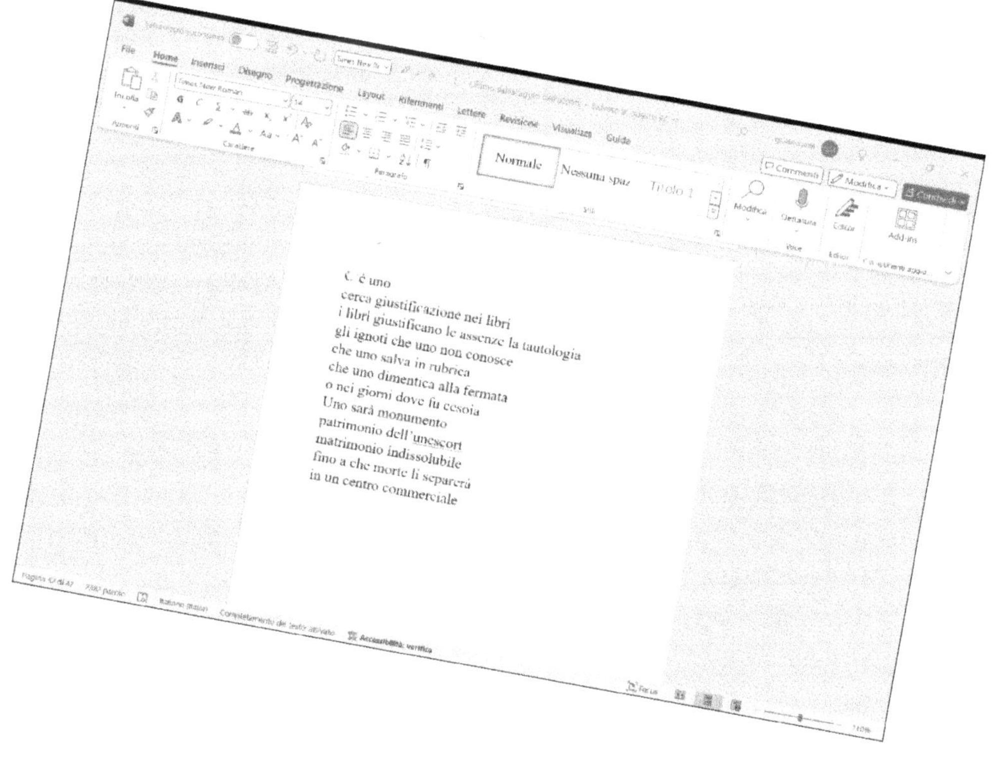
C' è uno
cerca giustificazione nei libri
i libri giustificano le assenze la tautologia
gli ignoti che uno non conosce
che uno salva in rubrica
che uno dimentica alla fermata
o nei giorni dove fu cesoia
Uno sarà monumento
patrimonio dell'unescort
matrimonio indissolubile
fino a che morte li separerà
in un centro commerciale

There is one
in books
absences tautology
one does not know
the address book
at the bus stop
when he was a shear
monument
unescorted
until death will separate them
in a shopping center

one
seeks
justification
in books

seeks justification
the books justify
the unknown that
that one saves in
that one forgets
or in the days
One will be a
heritage of
indissoluble marriage

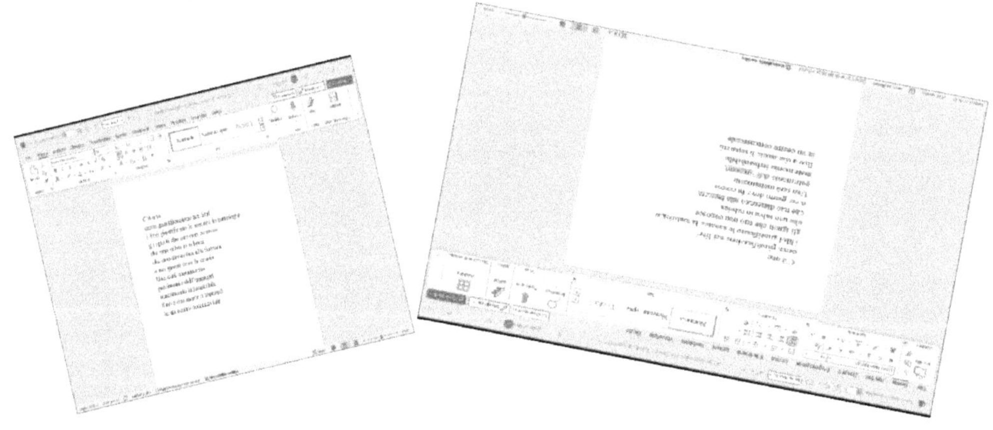

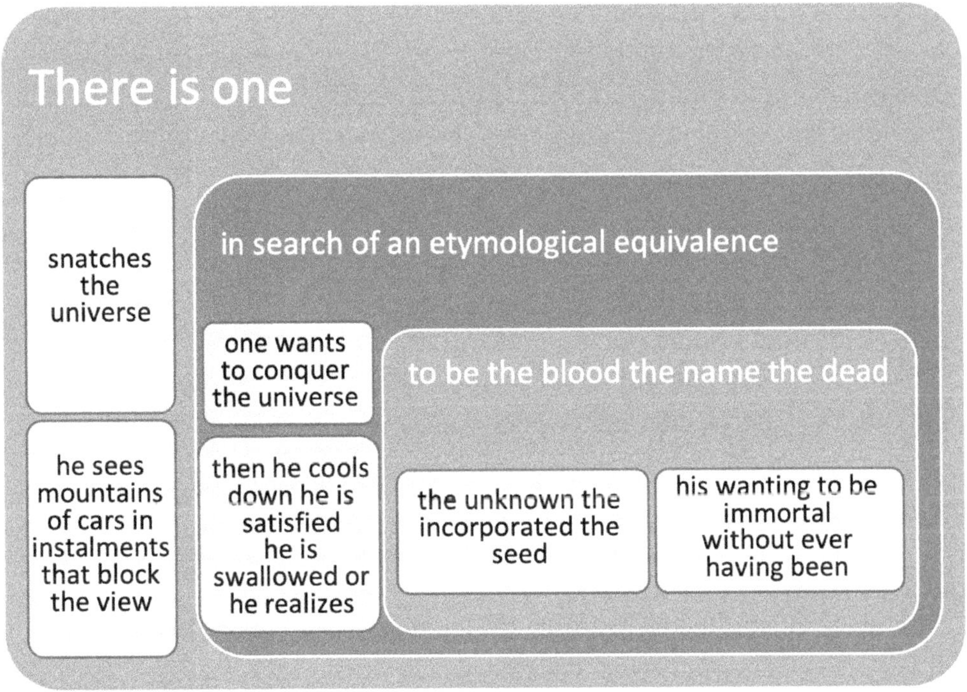

There is one

snatches the universe

he sees mountains of cars in instalments that block the view

in search of an etymological equivalence

one wants to conquer the universe

then he cools down he is satisfied
he is swallowed or he realizes

to be the blood the name the dead

the unknown the incorporated the seed

his wanting to be immortal without ever having been

There is one
delivers himself to the breakup with the unknowns
in the secrets of a childish project
where there are no banks clerks
variable rate mortgages
One says things
as if they really were things
especially in the evening among the pvc plates
In the morning one takes the bus again
and waits for the moment in which the question will arrive
sometimes hebdomadary other daily
One knows that the answer will be evasive
one knows by looking at his Swedish backabro
Today one is dust of time and planets
there are no names but the name lasts

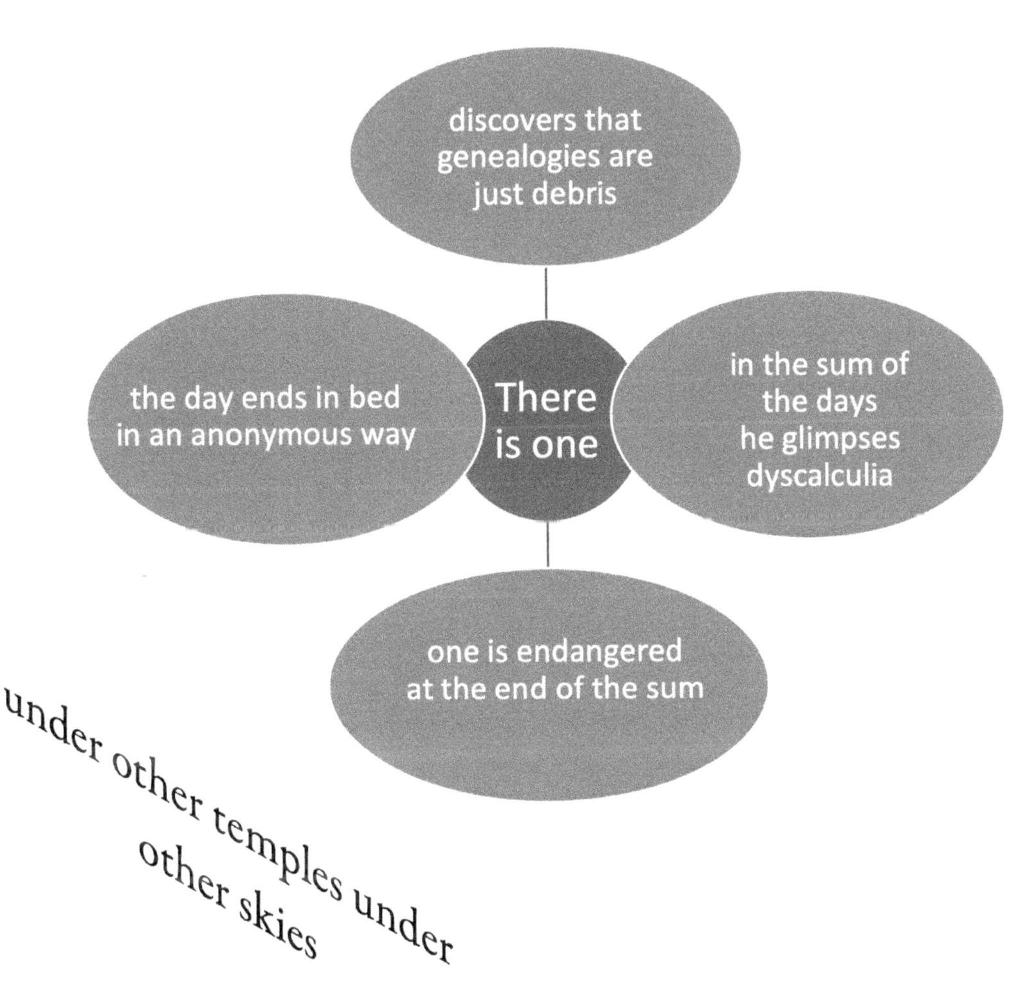
discovers that genealogies are just debris
the day ends in bed in an anonymous way
There is one
in the sum of the days he glimpses dyscalculia
one is endangered at the end of the sum
under other temples under other skies

There is one

he has not noticed that he has lived in comparison

a harmless minority adjective

the exegesis of a never-emerged unknown

One is
dominated by
banks
by the
ludopathy of
things in
instalments
he becomes a
monthly
payment
A chant pulled
out by the
forceps of
accounts
One can no
longer see
oneself
different from
he is seen

IV

(beliefs)

there was a wiser time when not
neither I nor you nor they existed; we were all the same
—C. Annino

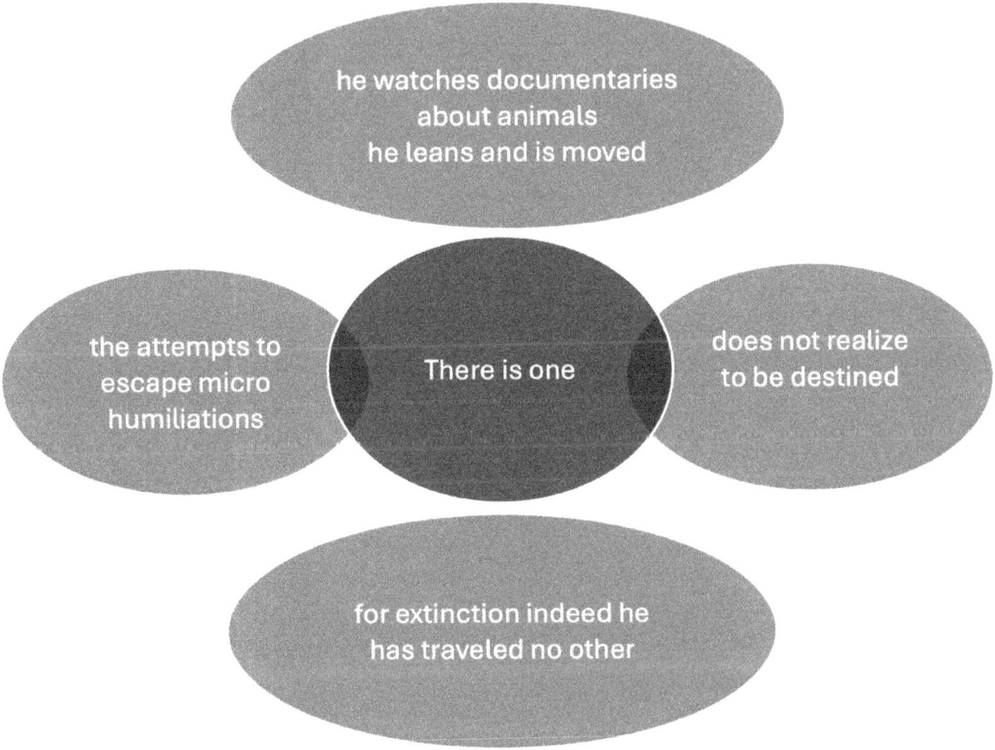

he watches documentaries
about animals
he leans and is moved

the attempts to
escape micro
humiliations

There is one

does not realize
to be destined

for extinction indeed he
has traveled no other

micro humiliations

<u>the main gesture of putting his hair in place</u>
<u>the footsteps arise from a parthenogenesis that does not lead to nothing</u>
<u>One gets distracted for a moment in the daily microcosm</u>
<u>just 30 or 40 years</u>

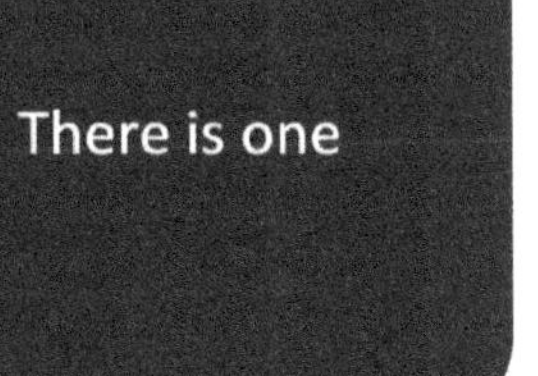

- In the intertwining of synapses and half-sleep he thinks that his father and grandmother
- died at the same age and that he has only twenty-five years left

Obviously he cannot measure them

- To count the events the things the naderías that can be thought but not expected
- He doesn't even remember what has or hasn't happened twenty-five years ago

One happens and does not remember descends below sea level while the unknowns with a nod of the head say always yes

- What could be missing now of that before that seems to have ended up in a concentration camp
- vanished dissolved lived as a particle of c 14 or a fracture of the midbrain

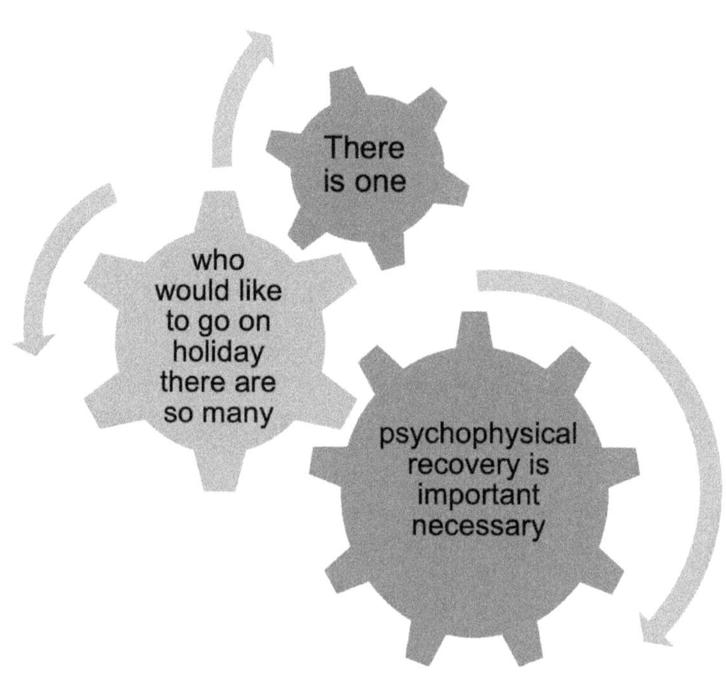

imposed by an indispensable law

One has only 15 days off a year
so he takes them in July
in August he will go back to the
office to take the bus with that
taste of sweat

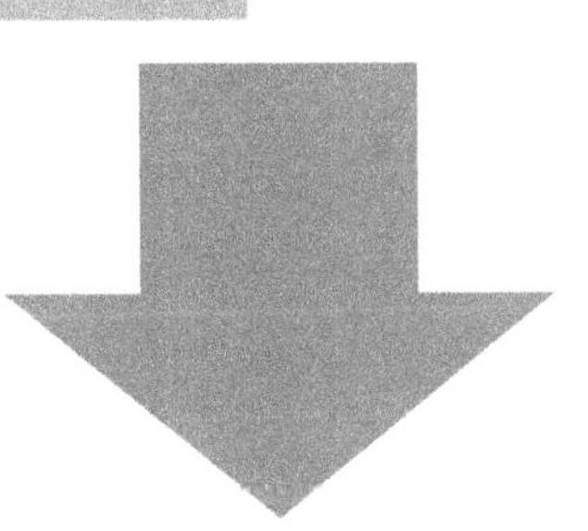

Everyone wants to go to holidays in
August One would like to go to
some nice place like La Rochelle
to fill up with Atlantic
but then decide to go to xxx
or in xxx with full board

One day to leave one to return

Thirteen days of vacation

Sometimes the unknowns believe they exist

There's one
watches the news a
report on refugees
He doesn't realize
that there are also
many
in the houses in the
villas in the anthills

They seek shelter
from the offices
from the
factories
from the lights of
the shops and
perfumeries

They take refuge on buses
inside every type of sheet
metal they commute by train
they are the furniture of
carriages

Many dead living men
believe or they hope for
something in the afterlife
they don't realize or can't
that it would only be to
meet again those who
they have pissed off here

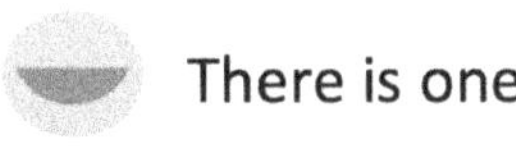

There is one

who takes the place of Al Khuwarizmi

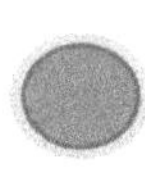

one is only an algorithm

Fooled by the false information received approximated to what he experienced in moments of distraction

He does not get out of it he does not understand he does not criticize he does not draw conclusion

Some people believe they exist

- Some people believe they exist
- Some people believe they exist
- Some people believe they exist
- Some people believe they exist
- Some people believe they exist

- Some people believe they exist
- Some people believe they exist
- Some people believe they exist
- Some people believe they exist
- Some people believe they exist
- Some people believe they exist
- Some people believe they exist
- Some people believe they exist
- Some people believe they exist
- Some people believe they exist
- Some people believe they exist
- Some people believe they exist

About the Author

Giulio R. M. Maffii was born in Florence, Italy. His practice spans poetry—linear, experimental and visual—and visual art. His work has been published internationally. He collaborates with the theatre company *Bubamara Teatro* and has taught for many years at the University of Florence. His works include the 2020 essay "The Feet Forward: The Long Walk of Anthropos and Thanatos between Poetry and Similar Vices" in *Archive for Anthropology and Ethnology*. His most recent work in visual poetry, *Sequenze per sbagliare il bersaglio* (2021), marks the first appearance of his combination of poetic language and "smart art," integrating collages, images, office graphics, drawings, and photography. In 2025 he presented the lecture "Archipoetry: Designing the Self from the 'Point' to the Metaverse," outlining the theoretical foundations of this experimental practice. His website https://giuliomaffii.com/

www.ingramcontent.com/pod-product-compliance
Ingram Content Group UK Ltd.
Pitfield, Milton Keynes, MK11 3LW, UK
UKHW062002290726
14090UKWH00022B/1351

9 798991 869294